Weight Watchers Freestyle 2018 Cookbook

The Ultimate Weight Watchers Freestyle Recipes for Weight Loss Fast

Freestyle Marsh

© Copyright 2017 –Freestyle Marsh- All Rights Reserved.

In no way is it legal to reproduce, duplicate, or transmit any part of this document by either electronic means or in printed format. Recording of this publication is strictly prohibited, and any storage of this material is not allowed unless with written permission from the publisher. All rights reserved.

The information provided herein is stated to be truthful and consistent, in that any liability, regarding inattention or otherwise, by any usage or abuse of any policies, processes, or directions contained within is the solitary and complete responsibility of the recipient reader. Under no circumstances will any legal liability or blame be held against the publisher for any reparation, damages, or monetary loss due to the information herein, either directly or indirectly.
Respective authors own all copyrights not held by the publisher.

Legal Notice:
This book is copyright protected. This is only for personal use. You cannot amend, distribute, sell, use, quote or paraphrase any part or the content within this book without the consent of the author or copyright owner. Legal action will be pursued if this is breached.

Disclaimer Notice:
Please note the information contained within this document is for educational and entertainment purposes only. Every

attempt has been made to provide accurate, up-to-date and reliable, complete information. No warranties of any kind are expressed or implied. Readers acknowledge that the author is not engaging in the rendering of legal, financial, medical or professional advice.

By reading this document, the reader agrees that under no circumstances are we responsible for any losses, direct or indirect, which are incurred as a result of the use of information contained within this document, including, but not limited to, errors, omissions, or inaccuracies.

Table of contents

Introduction 9

Chapter 1: Getting to Know the Basics of Weight Watcher Freestyle 11

    The origin of the Weight Watchers Diet 11

    The basics of the diet 13

    Is following the diet costly? 15

    Some advantages of the diet 16

    Some disadvantages of the diet 16

Chapter 2: Focusing on The Freestyle Program Itself 18

    Getting to know the mechanism behind Point System 18

    The unique changes for Freestyle 20

    Ultimate Tips for A Successful Weight Watchers Journey 22

Chapter 3: Having A Look at The Meal Plan 24

    Sample Freestyle Meal 24

Chapter 4: Breakfast Recipes 29

    Ricotta and Eggy Bread Tomatoes 29

Berryful Bowl of Granola 31

Amazing Bacon and Cheese Quiche 33

Extremely Healthy Banana Smoothie 35

Almond Berry Smoothie 36

Astonishing 3 Ingredients Pancake 38

Chapter 5: Soup Recipes 40

Generous Egg Drop Soup 40

Glorious Onion Soup 42

Deliciously Sour Thai Soup 44

Smart Emmenthal Soup... 46

Tuscan Veggie Soup 48

Generous Potato Soup... 50

Chapter 6: Meat Recipes 52

Potato and BBQ Chicken Slaw................................ 52

Berry Dredged Balsamic Chicken 54

Ravishing Orange Baked Chicken 56

A Math Addict's Roast Pork.................................... 58

Dreamy Chicken Curry 60

The Caramelized Pork Chops with Onion 62

Mustard Glazed Lamb Cutlets 64

Creative Mango Chicken 66

Costa Brava Chicken 68

The Original Southwestern Pork Chops 70

Delicious Piri Piri Chicken 72

Chapter 7: Seafood Recipes 74

Juicy Cod Fingers Burger 74

Secret Recipe Used Shrimp Scampi 76

Toasted Rye with Salmon and Avocado 78

The Mighty Prawn and Banana Salsa 80

Delightful Dijon Fish 82

Chapter 8: Salad Recipes 84

Nice and Cold Thai Salad 84

Turtle (And Human) Friendly Salad 86

Melon and Watercress Salad 88

Cute Cauliflower Salad 90

Orange and Onion Magnificent Salad 92

Avocado and Cilantro Medley 94

Chapter 9: Vegetarian/Vegan Recipes 96

Cha-Ching Tortilla Pizza 96

Vegan Butter Balls 98

Respectable Avocado Spread 99

Beet and Mushroom Avocado Salad 101

Magnificent Bean Balls 103

Crispy Potatoes with Vegan Sauce 105

Zucchini "Pizza" Fancy Boats 107

Friendly Heirloom Carrots 109

Chapter 10: Dessert Recipes 111

Fried Apple Slices 111

Easy to Make Carrot Balls 113

The Mean Green Smoothie 115

Very Zesty Lemon Cheesecake 117

Watermelon Sorbet 119

Palatable Carrot Cake 121

The Weight Watchers Brown Betty 123

Amazing Baked Apples 125

Rice Pudding and Golden Raisins 126

Conclusion 128

Appendix 129

    list of the most common ingredients and their SP (Old Program) 129

    Ingredients and Food Groups That are Zeroed Out in the new Freestyle Plan. 133

Introduction

Ever since its conception, the weight watchers diet had gained an extremely large popularity!

Having developed a friendly and extremely supportive community all around the world, the Weight Watchers program slowly became the prime diet for anyone who wanted to trim down their fat and stay healthy without sacrificing any of the favorite food from your list!

This is possible, thanks to the carefully crafted SmartPoint system.

Throughout the years, the diet has seen a number of different iterations of the points system that governs how the SmartPoints (Previously PlusPoints) are assigned to certain food groups.

Their latest update to this system is the "Weight Watcher Freestyle" program that seamlessly cuts down almost 200+ ingredients to 0 SmartPoint that gives you a much more versatile and flexible control over your diet.

That being said, I thank you for purchasing and downloading my book and I do hope that you will find the manuscript to be as helpful and useful as intended.

My aim with this book is to reach as wide of an audience as possible! Even if you are an absolute amateur in the field of Weight Watchers diet, I want this book to be your one stop shop for a quick briefing.

As such, this book has been divided into individual bite sized chapters that each focus on the fundamentals of the Weight Watchers program and Smart Points System, which are later on followed by the amazing assortment of recipes.

I realize that you might be extremely excited to jump into the recipes right now! But I highly encourage you to take some time to go through the introductory chapters in order to fully grasp the core concept of the topic of at hand.

Welcome, to the amazing world of Weight Watchers Freestyle!

Chapter 1: Getting to Know the Basics of Weight Watcher Freestyle

If you reading this book, then I do believe that you have already made up your mind and have decided to follow the path of the Weight Watchers and are interested in knowing more about the fabled "Freestyle" form of the diet.

So, let's jump right into it!

As mentioned in the above introductory section, before I let you go in to the amazing recipes Freestyle recipes in the book, I would high encourage you to take some time to go through the introductory chapters (even more so if you are beginner) to have a good understanding of the whole concept.

That being said, you should appreciate the fact that despite being an update version, the Freestyle still holds a lot of similarities to the original Weight Watchers diet.

So, before specifically talking about the Freestyle Weight Watchers diet, allow me to talk a little bit about the original Weight Watchers first.

The origin of the Weight Watchers Diet

Established in 1923 by a humble home maker who went by the name Jean Nidetch hailing from Brooklyn, NY! The backstory behind this amazing diet is actually really interesting.

To fully understand the origin of the diet though, you must first learn to appreciate the concept from Jean's point of view.

Why you ask?

Because Jean was herself an individual who had been constantly suffering from the hardship of obesity, and the Weight Watchers diet was the solution to her problem that helped her to control her food lust and trim down her body fat.

During her exploratory journey, she took various steps to trim down her fat by experiment with a number of different kinds of diet! And while in the end she was in: fact able to reach her goal, she soon discovered something very crucial that created the foundation of the Weight Watchers diet.

she soon had a sort of epiphany when she realizes that this is not a problem of her, but rather this is a problem, which is experienced by hundreds if not thousands of people on the planet!

Keeping that in mind though, she went out on a personal quest full of experimentations with multiple diets in order to find the best one that would help herself as well other individuals who are suffering from a similar situation.

During her experimentation, she was able to lose almost 9 Kilos of weight!

However, she soon realized that in the long run, just dieting won't solve the obesity problem! The main problem that led to millions of people suffering from obesity all around the world was "Lack of Control"

According to her experience, it doesn't really matter what diet you follow. If you are unable to control your food intake, then you will soon gain back all of your lost pounds!

Upon further inspection of this topic, she soon realized that this is a problem that is very common amongst obese people.

Keeping that in mind, she soon started to take an initiative and create a simple support group with her friends and families with a very simple goal in mind "Help others who are suffering from obesity and diet problems", which soon went on to become the "Weight Watchers Organization"

The Weight Watchers program that is followed today, The Freestyle Program in our case, is the evolutionary fruit of a concept that was laid down way back in the 1920s.

This is a form of diet that does not help you to only trim down your fat, but also improves your physical and psychological health.

The basics of the diet

Unlike most diets out there, Weight Watchers doesn't really need you to follow a very strict dietary regime that would eliminate all of your favorite food from your life!

Rather, this diet encourages you to make healthy food and life choices by implementing a very meticulously and beautifully crafted "Point" system that assigned each ingredients/food.

This food-oriented point system is further accompanied by a Physical Point system, but that is not the focus of our book!

Throughout the years, there have been various updates to the point system.

During the early days, the point system followed a simple PointsPlus regime that was later on updated to the SmartPoints system.

In 2018, the Weight Watchers Organization has rolled out their latest program dubbed "Freestyle Program"

Now keep in mind that the Freestyle Program still follows the previous created SmartPoint system, however the number of points that are assigned to certain food groups have been significantly altered to "0" in the Freestyle program.

The method of maintaining your dietary balance comes from counting these foods.

In the previous program, each individual was assigned a set number of daily points depending on various factor such as sex, height and others (including your target weight to be lost)

The Freestyle program follows the same method, but tweeked the formula slightly to ensure that the owners are able to enjoy maximum benefit from this diet.

I will be discussing more regarding the updated SmartPoints system in the second chapter of the book, in this chapter, there are two more things that I would like to share.

Is following the diet costly?

Since the choice of food of this diet largely depends on the individuals, it is therefore actually possible to keep the cost of the whole diet at very reasonable levels.

If you are interested in joining the weight loss community however, those don't cost that much either.

At the time of writing, the online membership had a fee of 17.5$ per month, which had an additional 29.95$ initiation fee.

On the other hand, you can also go for in: Person meetings with unlimited access for $39.95 which has its perks as well.

So, for getting the official support from the Weight Watchers community, you may expect a bill of 50:60$.

Keep in mind that these numbers are subject to change, and it is highly recommended that visit

www.weightwatchers.com to get an updated value of their current plans.

But everything said and done, the plan ultimately depends on you!

As for the meals themselves, since there is no dietary restriction, you are allowed to choose any ingredient that fits your budget and create a meal plan accordingly.

The only thing to keep in mind, is to "not" cross your daily SmartPoint limit.

In terms following the Freestyle Diet, the most important thing to remember is to not exceed your weekly allocated SmartPoints limit.

Some advantages of the diet

- The Weight Watchers program won't impose horrible food restrictions upon you
- Through the membership and meeting, you will be able to receive various cooking advices and nutritional tips while sharing your own experience
- Even kids are allowed to join the experience!
- The Smart Points system encourages to maintain your portions which will allow you to gradually and steadily lose your weight
- Through FitPoints, exercise is largely encouraged which helps to maintain a nice physique

Some disadvantages of the diet

- Some people might not feel comfortable in sharing their personal information in group meetings
- Keeping track of your SmartPoints all throughout the day might get tedious if you don't have the patience

- Weekly weight loss progress might discourage you as the changes won't be that drastic initially
- The freedom to eat might make it difficult for you to stay in control

Chapter 2: Focusing on The Freestyle Program Itself

As mentioned above, the earlier form of Point System for Weight Watchers diet was the Points Plus System, which was later on updated to Beyond the Scale in 2015 that included a means of measuring and incorporating calories, fat and fiber to the points.

In November 2017 though, various changes came to the plan that eventually became the plan that we follow today.

In the UK, this is known as the Flex Plan and in the US, it is known as the Freestyle Plan.

Food points are still calculated based on the same measurements as before and included calories, fat, sugar, carbs etc. but they follow the aforementioned SmartPoints program.

Essentially, the latest program is designed to encourage people to eat more lean protein sources such as turkey, chicken, egg, lentils and beans while cutting down on sugary or fatty foods.

Getting to know the mechanism behind Point System

If you have gone through the section above, you should have a good understanding of the program and understood that the point system is the beating heart of the Weight Watchers program.

Keep in mind that we will be using the "SmartPoints" version, which is an updated version of the previous PlusPoints system.

This refurbished plan allows an individual to sub: consciously create a meal plan that allows them to lean more towards a healthier lifestyle.

A simple formula for calculating the Smartpoints of your meal is done using the formula below.

Points = (Calories + (Fat x 4) - (Fiber x 10))/50

However, if you want greater accuracy, then you can always refer to the provided list of the common ingredients (and their SP) in the section below.

As for calculating your daily SmartPoints limit, there are actually a number of amazing calculators out there that will help you to achieve that. Two good examples are

http://www.healthyweightforum.org/eng/calculators/ww:points:allowed/

or

http://www.calculator.net/weight:watchers:points:calculator.html

Just to give you an idea though, if you are male of 20 years and have a weight of 70kgs with height of 5 feet and your target is to lose 10 kg, and then your allocated SP will be 30.

However, the best way to calculate your Daily and Weekly Allowance is still through the official Weight Watchers App that is provided upon availing your membership.

But if you want to experiment with the program for free, then the above-mentioned websites will be able to help you while the following apps will help you as well.

- Ultimate Food Diary App (This app is the only one that has been updated to provide services that resemble the Freestyle meal plan)
- iTrackBites (This is yet another app that is very close to the official WW app. However, this was doing not support the Freestyle program at the time of writing, but was supposed to be updated very soon)

This means that you are allowed to eat as much food as you want as long as you do not cross your daily allocated limit.

It should be kept in mind though that the System does not only govern food items! But also, physical activities that comes in the form of FitPoints.

Doing some light exercise alongside your Weight Watchers diet will exponentially increase the effectiveness of the diet.

The unique changes for Freestyle

When considering the Freestyle Points System, there are two a few crucial things that you should keep in mind.

- **The new "Zero" Point foods:** As you have seen in the previous chapter, this is perhaps the biggest change to the program. Various food items that previous had a significant number of points have been completely cut down to "Zero" points that gives you more freedom when designing the meal plans.

- **About SmartPoints:** The updated Freestyle program will still use the same method of calculation, however your daily SmartPoint allocation will change a bit to balance out the new foods that are all zeroed out now. If you are already a member of the Weight Watchers program, then you may be able to do this with through their designated app, or alternatively you may use the apps that are mentioned in the previous section.

- **Weekly Point Allowance:** Despite having a change in your daily point allowance, the weekly allowance will still remain the same. This means that you will be able to include more food and adjust your plans with greater flexibility.

- **Rollover Points:** This is yet another feature that is exclusive to the new program. This allows you to "Roll Over" a maximum of 4 unused daily points to the coming week and use them if you need! So, for example, assuming that you have weekly limit of 120 Smart Points, if you use 116 points in previous week, you will have a SmartPoint allocation of 124 points for the latter week. This is a good strategy to follow if you have any major upcoming events.

With the basics out of the way now, you are now ready to explore the recipes!

Don't forget to have a look at the appendix where I have included a list of various food ingredients and their accompanying SP.

Ultimate Tips for A Successful Weight Watchers Journey

- Learn how to maintain your portions. Having a good understanding of ounce, cup etc. is crucial to when creating your meal plan. You don't want to overshoot your meal portions as it might result in uneven results.
- Although the SmartPoints for the recipes are roughly calculated in this book using the provided outline (at the appendix), it is still recommended that you learn how to calculate the SmartPoints by yourself.
- Make sure to skip "Diet" soft drinks. While they might be free from unwanted calories, they still pack a good load of artificial sweeteners, which may lead to various medical issues.
- While practicing your portion control, you should never skip on exercise! Even if it is for 5-10 minutes, you should try not to avoid a brief daily exercise routine.

- When you are eating, try to split the meals if you are eating with someone. This will allow you to lower the amount of calorie that you are taking in.
- Learn to experiment with various ingredients and recipes! Use the recipe in this book as a source of inspiration and create your own meals!

Chapter 3: Having A Look at The Meal Plan

Below you will find a sample meal plan that should help you to come up with your own plan!

Keep in mind that the following is just a rough combination that is to act as a template for you! You are to calculate your own Weight Watchers Freestyle point and create your meal plan accordingly.

You may use the recipes found in this book or come up with your own creations following the ingredients guideline found in the appendix.

Sample Freestyle Meal

<u>Reference for Week 1 Shopping List</u>

For Breakfast

Recipe 1: Ricotta and Eggy Bread Tomatoes

- 4 medium raw whole eggs
- 4 tablespoons of skimmed milk
- 4 slices of whole meal bread
- 4 sprays cooking spray
- 9 ounce of cherry tomatoes

- 9-ounce Ricotta cheese

Recipe 2: Berryful Bowl Of Granola

- 1 ounce of Porridge oats
- 2 teaspoons of Maple Syrup
- Cooking spray as needed
- 4 medium Bananas
- 4 pots of Caramel Layered Fromager Frais
- 5 ounce of Fresh Fruit Salad such as strawberries, blueberries and raspberries
- ¼ ounce of pumpkin seeds
- ¼ ounce of sunflower seeds
- ¼ ounce of dry Chia seeds
- ¼ ounce of Desiccated coconut

Recipe 3: Amazing Bacon and Cheese Quiche

- 3 and a ½ ounce of raw Broccoli cut up into small florets
- 4 sprays of Calorie controlled cooking spray
- 3 rasher bacon medallions, raw and roughly chopped up
- 2 medium spring onions trimmed and sliced
- 2 and a ½ ounce of Reduce Fat Grated Cheese
- 2 medium raw whole eggs
- ½ a cup of skimmed milk
- 3 and a ½ ounce of low soft cheese

For Lunch

Recipe 1: Berry Dredged Balsamic Chicken

- 3 pieces of skinless and boneless chicken breast

- Salt as needed
- Black pepper as needed
- ¼ cup of all-purpose flour
- 2/3 cup of low fat chicken broth
- 1 and a ½ teaspoon of corn starch
- ½ a cup of low sugar raspberry preserve
- 1 and a ½ tablespoon of balsamic vinegar

Recipe 2: Hearty Salisbury Steak

- 1 pound of extra lean ground beef
- ¼ teaspoon of garlic powder
- ½ a teaspoon of kosher salt
- ¼ teaspoon of black pepper
- 8 ounces of sliced mushrooms
- ¼ cup of minced onion
- 1 teaspoon of dried thyme
- 2 tablespoon of dry sherry white wine
- 12 ounce of fat free beef gravy

Recipe 3: The Mighty Prawn and Banana Salsa

- 2 peeled and thinly sliced bananas
- 2 peeled, seeded and diced cucumbers
- ½ a cup of fresh mint leaves
- ½ a cup of fresh cilantro leaves
- 1 teaspoon of finely chopped fresh ginger root
- 1 fresh thinly sliced red Chile pepper
- ¼ cup of lime juice
- 1 tablespoon of fish sauce
- 1 tablespoon of brown sugar
- 1 and a ½ pound of peeled and deveined tiger prawns

For Dinner

Recipe 1: Dreamy Chicken Curry

- 2 cans of coconut milk
- 2 tablespoon of green curry paste
- 2/3 cup of chicken broth
- 1 can of 8 ounces sliced up water chestnuts (drained)
- 1 can of 8-ounce sliced bamboo shoots drained
- 1 piece of green bell pepper cut up into 1-inch pieces
- 1 cup of sliced fresh mushrooms
- 3 boneless chicken breasts cut up into 1-inch portions
- 3 tablespoon of fish sauce
- ¼ cup of chopped up fresh basil

Recipe 2: Toasted Rye with Salmon and Avocado

- ½ of a medium avocado
- 1 tablespoon of chopped fresh chives
- 2 teaspoon of lime juice
- ½ a teaspoon of chili flakes
- ½ teaspoon of chili flakes
- 2 slices of dark rye bread
- 1 medium fresh Lebanese cucumber (thinly slices)
- 5 ounces of smoked salmon
- 1 ounce of trimmed snow peas

Recipe 3: Friendly Heirloom Carrots

- 1 bunch of fine heirloom carrots
- 1 tablespoon of fresh thyme leaves
- ½ a tablespoon of coconut oil
- 1 tablespoon of date paste
- 1/8 cup of fresh squeeze orange juices
- 1/8 teaspoon of sea salt

- Salt as needed

Chapter 4: Breakfast Recipes

Ricotta and Eggy Bread Tomatoes

Serving: 4

Prep Time: 5 minutes

Cook Time: 10 minutes

SmartPoints: 3

Ingredients

- 4 medium raw whole eggs
- 4 tablespoons of skimmed milk
- 4 slices of wholemeal bread
- 4 sprays cooking spray
- 9-ounce of cherry tomatoes
- 9-ounce Ricotta cheese

How To

1. Lightly beat eggs and milk and season with black pepper
2. Take a shallow dish and add breads in layer
3. Pour egg mix over and turn the bread several times to coat
4. Take a large sized nonstick frying pan and place it over medium heat

5. Mist with cooking spray

6. Fry the breads in batches for about 2:3 minutes each side until golden

7. Cut the slices in half and keep them on the side

8. Add tomatoes to the pan and stir for 2:3 minutes

9. Serve the bread with tomatoes and ricotta

10. Enjoy!

Nutrition Values (Per Serving)

- Calories: 254
- Fat: 9g
- Carbohydrates: 34g
- Protein: 8g

Berryful Bowl of Granola

Serving: 6

Prep Time: 5 minutes

Cook Time: 25 minutes

SmartPoints: 2

Ingredients

- 1 ounce of Porridge oats
- 2 teaspoons of Maple Syrup
- Cooking spray as needed
- 4 medium Bananas
- 4 pots of Caramel Layered Fromager Frais
- 5 ounce of Fresh Fruit Salad such as strawberries, blueberries and raspberries
- ¼ ounce of pumpkin seeds
- ¼ ounce of sunflower seeds
- ¼ ounce of dry Chia seeds
- ¼ ounce of Desiccated coconut

How To

1. Preheat your oven to 302-degree Fahrenheit
2. Line up baking tray with baking paper
3. Take a large bowl and add oats, seeds, maple syrup
4. Spread the mixture out on the baking tray

5. Mix with coconut oil spray and bake for 20 minutes, making sure to keep stirring it from time to time

6. Sprinkle coconut at the 15 minutes point

7. Remove from the oven and spread out on cold baking tray

8. Slice bananas and layer in a bowl with Fromager Frais

9. Sprinkle granola on top and serve with the berries

10. Enjoy!

Nutrition Values (Per Serving)

- Calories: 446
- Fat: 29g
- Carbohydrates: 37g
- Protein: 13g

Amazing Bacon and Cheese Quiche

Serving: 4

Prep Time: 10 minutes

Cook Time: 30 minutes

SmartPoints: 4

Ingredients

- 3 and a ½ ounce of raw Broccoli cut up into small florets
- 4 sprays of Calorie controlled cooking spray
- 3 rasher bacon medallions, raw and roughly chopped up
- 2 medium spring onions trimmed and sliced
- 2 and a ½ ounce of Reduce Fat Grated Cheese
- 2 medium raw whole eggs
- ½ a cup of skimmed milk
- 3 and a ½ ounce of low soft cheese

How To

1. Preheat your oven to 356-degree Fahrenheit

2. Cook broccoli in a pan of boiling water over medium heat and cook for 4 minutes

3. Drain and spread out layers in kitchen paper and allow them to dry

4. Take a nonstick frying pan and place it over medium heat
5. Grease with cooking spray and add bacon and spring onions, cook for 4:5 minutes
6. Take a 7-inch shallow round cake and grease with cooking spray
7. Spread broccoli and bacon mix over the base and scatter cheese
8. Season with black pepper
9. Beat the eggs, milk, soft cheese together
10. Pour into the tin and bake for 25 minutes
11. Enjoy!

Nutrition Values (Per Serving)

- Calories: 365
- Fat: 24g
- Carbohydrates: 32g
- Protein: 4g

Extremely Healthy Banana Smoothie

Serving: 1

Prep Time: 5 minutes

Cook Time: 0 minutes

SmartPoints: 2

Ingredients

- 1 piece of banana
- 2 cups of chopped kale
- ½ a cup of light unsweetened almond milk
- 1 tablespoon of flax seed

How To

1. Add the listed ingredients to your blender and blend them
2. Once you have a smooth mixture, chill and serve!

Nutrition Values (Per Serving)

- Calories: 311
- Fat: 7g
- Carbohydrates: 56g
- Protein: 12g

Almond Berry Smoothie

Serving: 4

Prep Time: 10 minutes

Cook Time: 0 minutes

SmartPoints: 2

Ingredients

- 1 cup of frozen blueberries
- 1 piece of banana
- ½ a cup of almond milk
- 1 tablespoon of almond butter (Whole30 Compliant Brand)
- Water as needed

How To

1. Add the listed ingredients to the blender and blend them well until you have a smooth texture
2. Add water to thin out the smoothie
3. Chill and enjoy!

Nutrition Values (Per Serving)

- Calories: 321
- Fat: 11g

- Carbohydrates: 55g
- Protein: 5g

Astonishing 3 Ingredients Pancake

Serving: 1

Prep Time: 15 minutes

Cook Time: 10 minutes

SmartPoints: 2

Ingredients

- 1 small sized ripe banana
- 1 medium sized eggs
- 2 tablespoon of whole meal self-rising flour
- Cooking spray

How To

1. Take a medium sized bowl and add bananas, mash them using a fork

2. Whisk in eggs, flour and mix well to ensure that everything is incorporated well

3. Allow the mixture to sit for 5 minutes

4. Take a non-stick frying pan and grease up the pan with oil

5. Heat the pan over medium heat and spoon 2 tablespoon of your batter

6. Cook each side for 2 minutes until both sides are fully golden

7. Repeat with the remaining batter until they are used up

8. Enjoy!

Nutrition Values (Per Serving)

- Calories: 139
- Fat: 6g
- Carbohydrates: 18g
- Protein: 3g

Chapter 5: Soup Recipes

Generous Egg Drop Soup

Serving: 5

Prep Time: 5 minutes

Cook Time: 5 minutes

SmartPoints: 1

Ingredients

- 4 cups of low sodium chicken broth
- ½ a teaspoon of soy sauce
- ½ a cup of cooked, boneless and skinless chopped up chicken breast
- ½ a cup of frozen green peas
- ¼ cup of thinly sliced green onion
- 1 lightly beaten eggs

How To

1. Take a saucepan and place it over medium heat, add chicken stock and soy sauce

2. Bring the mix to a boil and add peas, green onions chicken and stir

3. Bring the mix to boil once again

4. Remove the heat and slowly drizzle in the egg
5. Wait for a minute until the egg sets in
6. Stir and ladle the soup into serving bowls
7. Enjoy!

Nutrition Values (Per Serving)

- Calories: 119
- Fat: 4g
- Carbohydrates: 8g
- Protein: 14g

Glorious Onion Soup

Serving: 4

Prep Time: 5 minutes

Cook Time: 25 minutes

SmartPoints: 4

Ingredients

- 2 large sized finely sliced onion
- 2 cups of vegetable stock
- 1 teaspoon of brown sugar
- 1 cup of red wine
- 1 measure of brandy
- 1 teaspoon of herbs de Provence
- 4 slices of stale bread
- 4 ounces of grated strong cheese
- 1 ounce of grated parmesan
- 1 tablespoon of plain flour
- 2 tablespoon of olive oil
- 1 ounce of butter
- Salt as needed
- Pepper as needed

How To

1. Take a pan and place it over medium-high heat

2. Add oil and butter and allow it to heat up

3. Add onion and sugar and keep cooking until the sugar dissolves and the onions are slightly caramelized

4. Pour brandy and flambé and stir well to dish out flames

5. Add flour and herbs de Provence and stir

6. Add stock and followed by gradual addition of the red wine

7. Season a bit and a lower down the heat to low

8. Simmer for 20 minutes, add a bit more water if needed to make it less thick

9. Ladle the soup into bowls

10. Place rounds of stale bread on top and add a bit of cheese

11. Garnish with some parmesan

12. Broil for just a bit to melt the cheese, serve!

Nutritional Values (Per Serving)

- Calories: 55
- Fat: 1.7g
- Carbohydrates: 8g
- Protein: 3.6g

Deliciously Sour Thai Soup

Serving: 4

Prep Time: 10 minutes

Cook Time: 15 minutes

SmartPoints: 1

Ingredients

- 3 cups of chicken stock
- 1 tablespoon of tom yum paste
- ½ a clove of finely chopped garlic clove
- 3 stalks of chopped lemon grass
- 2 kaffir lime leaves
- 2 skinless and boneless chicken breast all shredded up
- 4 ounces of thinly sliced mushrooms
- 1 tablespoon of fish sauce
- 1 tablespoon of lime juice
- 1 teaspoon of chopped green Chile pepper
- 1 bunch of chopped coriander
- 1 sprig of fresh basil (chopped up)

How To

1. Take a large sized saucepan and add chicken stock
2. Bring the mix to a boil
3. Stir in tom yum paste, garlic and cook for 2 minutes
4. Stir in lemon grass, kaffir lime leaves and simmer for 5 minutes over low heat

5. Add mushrooms, fish sauce, green Chile, lime juice, pepper and keep cooking over medium heat until blended well
6. Remove the heat and serve warm with a garnish of coriander and basil
7. Enjoy!

Nutrition Values (Per Serving)

- Fat: 1.8g
- Protein: 10g
- Carbohydrate: 5g
- Calories: 71

Smart Emmenthal Soup

Serving: 2

Prep Time: 5 minutes

Cook Time: 5 minutes

SmartPoints: 1

Ingredients

- 2 cups of cauliflower pieces
- 1 cubed up potato
- 2 cups of yeast free vegetable stock
- 3 tablespoons of cubed up Emmenthal cheese
- 2 tablespoons of fresh chives
- 1 tablespoon of pumpkin seeds
- 1 pinch of nutmeg
- 1 pinch of cayenne pepper

How To

1. *Take a pot and add vegetable broth, place it over medium heat and allow it to heat up*
2. *Add potatoes and cauliflower and cook them until tender*
3. *Transfer the veggies to a blender and puree*
4. *Return the pureed mixture to the broth and stir well*
5. *Season the soup with cayenne, nutmeg, salt and pepper*
6. *Add Emmenthal cheese, chives and stir*
7. *Garnish with pumpkin seed and enjoy!*

Nutrition Values (Per Serving)

- Calories: 351
- Fats: 14g
- Carbs: 28g
- Fiber: 4g

Tuscan Veggie Soup

Serving: 6

Prep Time: 15 minutes

Cook Time: 20 minutes

SmartPoints: 1

Ingredients

- 1 x 15 ounce can of low sodium cannellini beans (drained and rinsed)
- 1 tablespoon of olive oil
- ½ of a large sized onion diced up
- 2 diced up carrots
- 2 stalks of diced celery
- 1 small sized diced zucchini
- 1 minced garlic clove
- 1 tablespoon of chopped fresh thyme leaves
- 2 teaspoons of chopped fresh sage
- ½ a teaspoon of salt
- ¼ teaspoon of freshly ground black pepper
- 32 ounce of low sodium chicken broth
- 14 ounce of no salt diced tomatoes
- 2 cups of chopped baby spinach leaves
- 1/3 cup of freshly grated parmesan

How To

1. Take a small sized bowl and add beans and mash using spoon
2. Keep the mashed beans on the side
3. Take a large sized soup pot and place it over medium heat
4. Add oil and allow the oil to heat up
5. Add onion, carrots, celery, garlic, zucchini, thyme, ½ a teaspoon of salt, sage, ¼ teaspoon of pepper and cook for 5 minutes until the veggies are soft
6. Add broth and tomatoes (with the juice) and bring to a boil
7. Add the mashed beans and any whole beans and stir
8. Add spinach and stir for 3 minutes
9. Cook until the spinach has wilted
10. Serve with a garnish of parmesan and enjoy!

Nutrition Values (Per Serving)

- Calories: 145
- Fat: 4g
- Carbohydrates: 21g
- Protein: 8g

Generous Potato Soup

Serving: 4-6

Prep Time: 5 minutes

Cook Time: 28 minutes

SmartPoints: 2

Ingredients

- 2 tablespoon of extra virgin olive oil
- 1 chopped large sized onion
- 2 crushed cloves of garlic
- 1 pound of sweet potato, peeled and cut up into medium pieces
- ½ a teaspoon of ground cumin
- ¼ teaspoon of ground chili
- ½ a teaspoon of ground coriander
- ¼ teaspoon of ground cinnamon
- ¼ teaspoon of salt
- 2 cups of chicken stock
- Low fat crème fraiche
- Freshly chopped parsley
- Coriander as needed

How To

1. Take a large sized pan and place it over medium high heat
2. Add olive oil and heat it up

3. Add onions and Saute them until they are slightly browned
4. Turn down the heat to medium and add garlic and keep cooking for 2-3 minutes more
5. Add sweet potato and Saute for 3-4 minutes
6. Add the remaining spices and season with some salt
7. Cook for 2 minutes
8. Pour stock and turn the heat up
9. Bring the mixture to a boil and give it a stir
10. Put a lid on top and lower down the lid and bring it to a slow simmer
11. Cook for 20 minutes until the potatoes are tender
12. Remove the pan from the heat
13. Take an immersion blender and puree the whole mixture
14. Add a bit of water if the soup is too thick
15. Check the soup for seasoning
16. Ladle the soup into your serving bowls
17. Give a swirl of crème fraiche
18. Sprinkle some chopped up parsley
19. Enjoy!

Nutrition Values (Per Serving)

- Calories: 324
- Fat: 7g
- Carbohydrates: 25g
- Protein: 12g

Chapter 6: Meat Recipes

Potato and BBQ Chicken Slaw

Serving: 1

Prep Time: 5 minutes

Cook Time: 45 minutes

SmartPoints: 2

Ingredients

- 1 medium sized raw Sweet Potato
- 1 medium skinless and raw chicken breast
- BBQ sauce as needed
- 1 tablespoon of low fat Mayonnaise
- 1 tablespoon of natural Greek yogurt
- 1 teaspoon of fresh lemon juice
- 1 and a ¾ ounce of finely shredded cabbage
- 1 ounce of grated raw carrots
- 1 medium spring onions finely sliced

How To

1. Preheat your oven to 352-degree Fahrenheit
2. Prick the potato skin with fork and place them on a baking tray, roast for 40:45 minutes

3. Take a ovenproof dish and add chicken and 2 tablespoon of water

4. Cover tightly with foil and bake for 25 minutes

5. Drain the cooking juice and cover the chicken with BBQ sauce

6. Turn well and coat it

7. Recover and bake for 15 minutes more

8. Take a bowl and add mayonnaise, yogurt, lemon juice and season with black pepper

9. Stir in cabbage, spring onion and carrot

10. Shred the chicken using 2 forks

11. Make a deep cut on top of the potato and top with chicken

12. Serve with the sale and enjoy!

Nutrition Values (Per Serving)

- Calories: 472
- Fat: 26g
- Carbohydrates: 36g
- Protein: 24g

Berry Dredged Balsamic Chicken

Serving: 4

Prep Time: 10 minutes

Cook Time: 20 minutes

SmartPoints: 3

Ingredients

- 3 pieces of skinless and boneless chicken breast
- Salt as needed
- Black pepper as needed
- ¼ cup of all-purpose flour
- 2/3 cup of low fat chicken broth
- 1 and a ½ teaspoon of corn starch
- ½ a cup of low sugar raspberry preserve
- 1 and a ½ tablespoon of balsamic vinegar

How To

1. Cut the chicken into bite sized portions and season with salt and pepper

2. Dredge the meat into flour and shake off excess

3. Take a non-stick skillet and place it over medium heat

4. Add chicken and cook for 15 minutes, turn once halfway through

5. Remove cooked chicken and transfer to plate

6. Add cornstarch, chicken broth, raspberry preserve into the skillet and stir in balsamic vinegar (keep the heat on medium)
7. Transfer the cooked chicken to the skillet
8. Cook for 15 minutes more, making sure to turn once
9. Serve and enjoy!

Nutrition Values (Per Serving)

- Calories: 546
- Fat: 35g
- Carbohydrates: 11g
- Protein: 44g

Ravishing Orange Baked Chicken

Serving: 4

Prep Time: 20 minutes

Cook Time: 35 minutes

SmartPoints: 2

Ingredients

- 2 tablespoon of orange juice
- 2 tablespoon of Dijon mustard
- ¼ teaspoon of salt
- ¾ cup of crumbled whole wheat crackers
- 1 tablespoon of grated orange zest
- 1 finely chopped shallot
- ¼ teaspoon of freshly ground black pepper
- 12 ounce of boneless and skinless chicken thigh

How To

1. Pre-heat your oven to a temperature of 350-degree Fahrenheit

2. Take a non-stick baking sheet and spray it with cooking spray

3. Take a small bowl and combine orange juice, salt and mustard

4. Take a sheet of wax paper and combine cracker crumbs, shallot, orange zest and pepper

5. Brush up the chicken with the mustard mix and dredge the chicken in the crumbs

6. Firmly place the crumbs to coat all sides of the chicken

7. Place the chicken on your baking sheet

8. Bake for about 15 minutes, making sure to turn it over

9. Bake for another 15 minutes more

10. Serve!

Nutrition Values (Per Serving)

- Calories: 194
- Fat: 7g
- Carbohydrates: 15g
- Protein: 19g

A Math Addict's Roast Pork

Serving: 8

Prep Time: 5 minutes

Cook Time: 30 minutes

SmartPoints: 3

Ingredients

- 1 cooking spray
- 2 teaspoons of dried thyme
- 2 teaspoons of dried oregano
- 1 teaspoon of garlic powder
- 1 teaspoon of onion powder
- 1 teaspoon of table salt
- 1 teaspoon of freshly ground black pepper
- 2 teaspoons of olive oil
- 2 pound of lean pork tenderloin

How To

1. Pre-heat your oven to a temperature of 400-degree Fahrenheit

2. Take a shallow roasting pan and coat it up with cooking spray

3. Take a small sized bowl and add thyme, garlic powder, oregano, pepper, salt and onion powder

4. Keep it aside

5. Gently rub oil all over the pork

6. Sprinkle the thyme mix all over the pork and transfer it to your prepared pa

7. Roast it up for 30 minutes until an instant read thermometer gives a reading of 160-degree Fahrenheit

8. Let it stand for about 10 minutes to cool it down

9. Slice it up using a crosswise into thin slices of about ½ inch thick slices

Nutrition Values (Per Serving)

- Calories: 151
- Fat: 5g
- Carbohydrates: 1g
- Protein: 24g

Dreamy Chicken Curry

Serving: 6

Prep Time: 10 minutes

Cook Time: 20 minutes

SmartPoints: 2

Ingredients

- 2 cans of coconut milk
- 2 tablespoon of green curry paste
- 2/3 cup of chicken broth
- 1 can of 8 ounces sliced up water chestnuts (drained)
- 1 can of 8-ounce sliced bamboo shoots drained
- 1 piece of green bell pepper cut up into 1-inch pieces
- 1 cup of sliced fresh mushrooms
- 3 boneless chicken breasts cut up into 1 inch portions
- 3 tablespoon of fish sauce
- ¼ cup of chopped up fresh basil

How To

1. Take a skillet and place it over medium heat

2. Add coconut milk and curry past, whisk

3. Simmer for 5 minutes

4. Stir in chicken broth, water chestnuts, bamboo shoots, bell pepper, mushroom and chicken

5. Season accordingly and add fish sauce
6. Add basil and stir
7. Simmer for 10 minutes
8. Serve and enjoy!

Nutrition Values (Per Serving)

- Calories: 416
- Fat: 33g
- Dietary Fiber: 1g
- Protein: 291g

The Caramelized Pork Chops with Onion

Serving: 4

Prep Time: 5 minutes

Cook Time: 40 minutes

SmartPoints: 3

Ingredients:

- 4 pound of chuck roast
- 4 ounces of green chopped green Chile
- 2 tablespoons of chili powder
- ½ a teaspoon of dried oregano
- ½ a teaspoon of ground cumin
- 2 minced garlic cloves
- Salt as needed

How To

1. Rub the chops with seasoning of 1 teaspoon of pepper and 2 teaspoons of salt
2. Take a skillet and place it over medium heat, add oil and allow the oil to heat up
3. Brown the seasoned chop both sides
4. Add water and onion to the skillet and cover, lower down the heat to low and simmer for 20 minutes

5. Turn the chops over and season with more salt and pepper
6. Cover and cook until the water fully evaporates and the beef shows a slightly brown texture
7. Remove the chops and serve with a topping of the caramelized onion
8. Serve and enjoy!

<u>Nutrition Values (Per Serving)</u>

- Calories: 47
- Fat: 3.5g
- Carbohydrates: 4g
- Protein: 0.5g

Mustard Glazed Lamb Cutlets

Serving: 4

Prep Time: 10 minutes

Cook Time: 10 minutes

SmartPoints: 3

Ingredients

- 1 tablespoon of Dijon mustard
- 1 tablespoon of honey
- 2 tablespoon of white wine vinegar
- 480g of trimmed lamb cutlet with fat trimmed
- 250g of cooked brown quick rice
- 2 cups of finely shredded baby spinach leaves

How To

1. Take a small sized bowl and add mustard, honey, vinegar and mix well
2. Pre-heat your BBQ grill to high
3. Cook the cutlets for about 2 minutes per side to ensure that they are cooked well
4. Brush half of your mustard mix near the end of the cooking
5. Take a microwave safe bowl and add the rice, place them in your microwave and cook
6. Stir in spinach leaves while the rice is hot

7. Divide the rice amongst your serving plates and top up with the grille cutlets

8. Drizzle the remaining mustard mix on top and enjoy!

Nutrition Values (Per Serving)

- Calories: 1570
- Fat: 126g
- Carbohydrates: 55g
- Protein: 54g

Creative Mango Chicken

Serving: 4

Prep Time: 25 minutes

Cook Time: 10 minutes

SmartPoints: 2

Ingredients

- 2 medium sized peeled and sliced mangoes
- 10 ounce of coconut milk
- 4 teaspoon of vegetable oil
- 4 teaspoon of spicy curry paste
- 14 ounce of skinless and boneless chicken breast halves cut up into cubes
- 4 medium sized shallots
- 1 large sized English cucumber (seeded and sliced)

How To

1. Slice half of the mangoes and add the halves to a bowl

2. Add mangoes and coconut milk to a blender and blend until you have a smooth puree

3. Keep the mixture on the side

4. Tae a large sized pot and place it over medium heat, add oil and allow the oil to heat up

5. Add curry paste and cook for 1 minute until you have a nice fragrance, add shallots and chicken to the pot and cook for 5 minutes

6. Pour mango puree to the mix and allow it to heat up

7. Serve the cooked chicken with mango puree and cucumbers

8. Enjoy!

Nutrition Values (Per Serving)

- Calories: 398
- Fat: 20g
- Carbohydrates: 31g
- Protein: 26g

Costa Brava Chicken

Serving: 4

Prep Time: 5 minutes

Cook Time: 25 minutes

SmartPoints: 2

Ingredients

- 1 can of 20 ounce of Pineapple chunks
- 10 skinless and boneless chicken breast halves
- 1 tablespoon of vegetable oil
- 1 teaspoon of ground cumin
- 1 teaspoon of ground cinnamon
- 2 minced garlic cloves
- 1 quartered onion
- 1 can of 14-ounce stewed tomatoes
- 2 cups of black olive
- ½ a cup of salsa
- 2 tablespoons of water
- 1 thinly sliced red bell pepper
- Salt as needed

How To

1. Drain the pineapples and reserve the juice
2. Sprinkle with some salt

3. Take a large sized frying pan and place it over medium heat
4. Add oil and allow the oil to heat up
5. Add cinnamon, cumin and sprinkle it all over
6. Add garlic and onion and cook until tender
7. Add the reserved pineapple juice, salsa, olives and tomatoes
8. Cover it up and allow it to simmer for 25 minutes
9. Take a bowl and add cornstarch and water
10. Stir the mixture into pan
11. Add bell pepper and simmer for a little longer until the sauce boils and thickens
12. Stir in pineapple chunks and thoroughly heat it up
13. Enjoy

Nutritional Values (Per Serving)

- Calories: 239
- Fat: 6g
- Carbohydrates: 1g
- Protein: 28g

The Original Southwestern Pork Chops

Serving: 4

Prep Time: 2 minutes

Cook Time: 13 minutes

SmartPoints: 3

Ingredients

- Vegetable cooking oil spray
- 4 ounce of boneless pork loin chop trimmed off its fat
- 1/3 cup of salsa
- 2 tablespoon of fresh lime juice
- ¼ cup of fresh cilantro (chopped)

How To

1. Take a large sized non-stick skillet and spray it with cooking spray

2. Heat it up until hot over high eat

3. Press the chops with your palm to flatten them slightly

4. Add them to the skillet and cook on 1 minute for each side until they are nicely browned

5. Lower down the heat to medium-low

6. Combine the salsa and lime juice

7. Pour the mix over the chops

8. Simmer uncovered for about 8 minutes until the chops are perfectly done
9. If needed, sprinkle some cilantro on top
10. Serve!

Nutrition Values (Per Serving)

- Calories: 184
- Fat: 8g
- Carbohydrates: 2g
- Protein: 25g

Delicious Piri Piri Chicken

Serving: 2

Prep Time: 10 minutes

Cook Time: 35 minutes

SmartPoints: 2

Ingredients

- 6 ounces of raw potato cut up in wedges
- 4 sprays of cooking spray
- 1 medium chicken breast, skinless and raw
- 1 sachet of Spicy Piri Piri Sauce
- 1 medium corn on the cob
- 1 medium wholemeal pitta bread
- 1 portion of mixed vegetable salad (veggies of your choice)
- 5 tablespoons of natural Greek yogurt
- 1 teaspoon of mint sauce

How To

1. Preheat your oven to 392-degree Fahrenheit
2. Put wedges on a baking tray and mist with cooking spray
3. Bake for 35 minutes
4. Add chicken on a chopping board and slice the fillet half lengthwise, making sure to opening by the middle

5. Place Clingfilm on either side of the chicken and bash with a rolling pin
6. Transfer to a dish and cover with Piri Piri sauce
7. Keep it on the side and allow it to sit for 15 minutes
8. Take a nonstick frying pan and place it over medium heat
9. Mist with cooking spray
10. Add corn and cook for 10 minutes
11. Turn off until the kernels are slightly charred
12. Mist the pan with more cooking spray and add the chicken, cook for minutes making sure to turn it halfway until fully cooked
13. Sprinkle pitta with a few drops water and bake for 3-4 minutes until they puff up
14. Take another bowl and mix yogurt and mint sauce
15. Slice the chicken, split the pitta and fill the pita with chicken and salad
16. Drizzle yogurt dressing on top and serve with corn, salad and wedges
17. Enjoy!

Nutrition Values (Per Serving)

- Calories: 533
- Fat: 21g
- Carbohydrates: 54g
- Protein: 35g

Chapter 7: Seafood Recipes

Juicy Cod Fingers Burger

Serving: 2

Prep Time: 15 minutes

Cook Time: 40 minutes

SmartPoints: 1

Ingredients

- 4 sprays of cooking spray
- 4 ounces of raw peeled parsnips
- 4 ounces of peeled raw carrots
- 1 medium sweet potato
- 1 medium raw egg whole, lightly beaten
- 8 ounces of raw cod
- 6 ounces of frozen peas
- 1 slice of lemon cut up into 4 wedges
- Chickpea shells/ bread crumbs for coating the fish

How To

1. *Preheat your oven to 392-degree Fahrenheit*
2. *Take 2 baking trays and mist with cooking spray*
3. *Cut parsnips, carrots and sweet potatoes into chips*

4. Transfer them to one cooking tray and mist with cooking spray

5. Roast for 40 minutes until golden, making sure to turn them halfway through

6. Crush the chickpea shells/bread crumbs with a rolling pin and transfer to a shallow dish

7. Put egg in another shallow dish

8. Cut the cod in 8 thick fingers and dip them in the egg and then in the crushed chick peas/bread crumbs

9. Put the crumbled fish on the second tray and bake for 15 minutes

10. Cook the peas in a pan of boiling water for 4 minutes

11. Drain and serve with the fish fingers, lemon wedges and chips

12. Enjoy!

Nutrition Values (Per Serving)

- Calories: 824
- Fat: 59g
- Carbohydrates: 22g
- Protein: 52g

Secret Recipe Used Shrimp Scampi

Serving: 4

Prep Time: 25 minutes

Cook Time: 0 minutes

SmartPoints: 1

Ingredients

- 4 teaspoon of olive oil
- 1 and a ¼ pound of medium shrimp
- 6-8 pieces of minced garlic cloves
- ½ a cup of low-sodium chicken broth
- ½ a cup of dry white wine
- ¼ cup of fresh lemon juice
- ¼ cup of fresh parsley + 1 tablespoon extra (all minced)
- ¼ teaspoon of salt
- ¼ teaspoon of freshly ground black pepper
- 4 slices of lemon

How To

1. Take a large sized bowl and place it over medium-high heat
2. Add oil and allow the oil to heat up
3. Add shrimp and cook for 2-3 minutes
4. Add garlic and cook for 30 seconds

5. Take a slotted spoon and carefully transfer the cooked shrimp to your serving platter

6. Add broth, lemon juice, wine, ¼ cup of parsley, salt and pepper to the same skillet and bring the whole mix to a boil

7. Keep boiling until the sauce has been reduced to half

8. Spoon the sauce over the cooked shrimp

9. Garnish with a bit of parsley and lemon

10. Serve and enjoy!

Nutrition Values (Per Serving)

- Calories: 184
- Fat: 6g
- Carbohydrates: 6g
- Protein: 55g

Toasted Rye with Salmon and Avocado

Serving: 2

Prep Time: 10 minutes

Cook Time: 0 minutes

SmartPoints: 1

Ingredients

- ½ of a medium avocado
- 1 tablespoon of chopped fresh chives
- 2 teaspoon of lime juice
- ½ a teaspoon of chili flakes
- ½ teaspoon of chili flakes
- 2 slices of dark rye bread
- 1 medium fresh Lebanese cucumber (thinly slices)
- 5 ounces of smoked salmon
- 1 ounce of trimmed snow peas

How To

1. Take a small sized bowl and add avocados, chives, chili and juice

2. Take a fork and mash everything until you have a smooth mixture

3. Season with some freshly ground black pepper and salt

4. Toast your bread carefully to ensure that you don't burn them

5. Spread the avocado mix over the toast and serve with some cucumber, salmon, pea shoot
6. Enjoy!

Nutrition Values (Per Serving)

- Calories: 194
- Fat: 19g
- Carbohydrates: 4g
- Protein: 3g

The Mighty Prawn and Banana Salsa

Serving: 4

Prep Time: 15 minutes

Cook Time: 3 minutes

SmartPoints: 2

Ingredients

- 2 peeled and thinly sliced bananas
- 2 peeled, seeded and diced cucumbers
- ½ a cup of fresh mint leaves
- ½ a cup of fresh cilantro leaves
- 1 teaspoon of finely chopped fresh ginger root
- 1 fresh thinly sliced red chile pepper
- ¼ cup of lime juice
- 1 tablespoon of fish sauce
- 1 tablespoon of brown sugar
- 1 and a ½ pound of peeled and deveined tiger prawns

How To

1. Take a large sized bowl and add bananas, cucumber, cilantro, ginger, red chile pepper and mix everything well
2. The above mix is your Salsa
3. Take a small sized bowl and add lime juice, brown sugar, fish sauce, sugar and blend
4. Add salsa mix to the fish sauce mix and stir
5. Take large saucepan and add salted water

6. Bring the water to a boil
7. Add prawns into the water and cook for 3 minutes
8. Serve the cooked prawn with banana salsa
9. Enjoy!

Nutrition Values (Per Serving)

- Fat: 2g
- Protein: 36g
- Carbohydrate: 25g
- Calories: 280

Delightful Dijon Fish

Serving: 2

Prep Time: 3 minutes

Cook Time: 12 minutes

SmartPoints: 2

Ingredients

- 1 piece of perch, flounder or sole fillet
- 1 tablespoon of Dijon mustard
- 1 and a ½ teaspoon of lemon juice
- 1 teaspoon of reduced sodium Worcestershire sauce
- 2 tablespoon of Italian seasoned bread crumbs
- 1 butter flavored cooking spray

How To

1. Preheat your oven to 450-degree Fahrenheit
2. Take a 11 x 7-inch baking dish and arrange your fillets carefully
3. Take a small sized bowl and add lemon juice, Worcestershire sauce, mustard and mix it well
4. Pour the mix over your fillet
5. Sprinkle a good amount of breadcrumbs
6. Bake for 12 minutes until fish flakes off easily
7. Cut the fillet in half portions and enjoy!

Nutrition Values (Per Serving)

- Calories: 125
- Fat: 2g
- Carbohydrates: 6g
- Protein: 21g

Chapter 8: Salad Recipes

Nice and Cold Thai Salad

Serving: 4

Prep Time: 10 minutes

Cook Time: 25 minutes

SmartPoints: 1

Ingredients

- 2 small zucchini pieces
- 1 small cucumber
- 2 peeled and shredded carrots
- ½ a cup of mung bean sprouts
- ¼ cup of chopped cashews
- ¼ cup of chopped fresh cilantro
- ½ a cup of sunshine sauce

For Sauce

- ½ a cup of unsweetened sunflower seed butter
- ½ a cup of coconut milk
- 1 lime juiced
- 1 tablespoon of coconut amino
- 1 minced garlic clove
- ½ a teaspoon of crushed red pepper flakes
- ½ a teaspoon of rice vinegar

How To

1. Add the sauce ingredients to a small bowl and mix
2. Peel the zucchini using peeler and julienne into long slices
3. Keep peeling until all four sides are peeled
4. Keep repeating the process with remaining zucchini and cucumbers
5. Add the noodles to a medium mixing bowl and add shredded carrots, bean sprouts, chopped cashews and cilantro
6. Allow it to chill for 30 minutes
7. Add a tablespoon of water to the sauce and take the sauce out
8. Pour it over salad and garnish with cilantro and cashews
9. Toss and enjoy!

Nutrition Values (Per Serving)

- Calories: 187
- Fat: 12g
- Carbohydrates: 19g
- Protein: 4g

Turtle (And Human) Friendly Salad

Serving: 6

Prep Time: 5 minutes

Cook Time: 5 minutes

SmartPoints: 1

Ingredients

- 1 chopped up heart of Romaine lettuce
- 3 diced Roma tomatoes
- 1 dice English cucumber
- 1 small sized red onions
- ½ a cup of curly parsley, finely chopped up
- 2 tablespoon of virgin olive oil
- Juice of ½ a large lemon
- 1 teaspoon of garlic powder
- Salt as needed
- Pepper as needed

How To

1. Wash the vegetables thoroughly under cold water
2. Prepare them by chopping, dicing or mincing as needed
3. Take a large salad bowl and transfer the prepped veggies
4. Add vegetable oil, olive oil, lemon juice and spice
5. Toss well to coat
6. Serve chilled if preferred

7. Enjoy!

Nutrition Values (Per Serving)
- Calories: 200
- Fat: 8g
- Carbohydrates: 18g
- Protein: 10g

Melon and Watercress Salad

Serving: 4

Prep Time: 15 minutes

Cook Time: 20 minutes

SmartPoints: 1

Ingredients

- 3 tablespoon of fresh lime juice
- 1 teaspoon of date paste
- 1 teaspoon of minced fresh ginger root
- ¼ cup of vegetable oil
- 2 bunch of chopped up and trimmed watercress
- 2 and a ½ cups of cubed watermelon
- 2 and a ½ cups of cubed cantaloupe
- 1/3 cup of toasted and sliced almonds

How To

1. Take a large sized bowl and add lime juice, ginger, date paste
2. Whisk well and add oil
3. Season with pepper and salt
4. Add watercress, watermelon
5. Toss well
6. Transfer to a serving bowl and garnish with sliced almonds
7. Enjoy!

Nutrition Values (Per Serving)

- Calories: 274
- Fat: 20g
- Carbohydrates: 21g
- Protein: 7g

Cute Cauliflower Salad

Serving: 2

Prep Time: 8 minutes

Cook Time: 0 minutes

SmartPoints: 1

Ingredients

- 1 head of cauliflower, broken up into bite sized pieces
- 1 small sized onion chopped up
- 1/8 cup of extra virgin olive oil
- ¼ cup of apple cider vinegar
- ½ a teaspoon of sea salt
- ½ a teaspoon of black pepper
- ¼ cup of dried cranberries
- ¼ cup of pumpkin seeds

How To

1. *Wash up and break your cauliflower into bite sized portions and add them to a bowl*
2. *Whisk oil, vinegar, salt and pepper in another bowl*
3. *Add pumpkin seeds, dried cranberries and the prepare dressing to your cauliflower*
4. *Add onion and toss well*
5. *Allow it to chill overnight*
6. *Serve and enjoy!*

Nutrition Values (Per Serving)

- Calories: 163
- Fat: 11g
- Carbohydrates: 16g
- Protein: 3g

Orange and Onion Magnificent Salad

Serving: 2

Prep Time: 15 minutes

Cook Time: 15 minutes

SmartPoints: 2

Ingredients

- 6 large pieces of oranges
- 3 tablespoon of red wine vinegar
- 6 tablespoon of olive oil
- 1 teaspoon of dried oregano
- 1 red onion thinly sliced up
- 1 cup of olive oil
- ¼ cup of chopped fresh chives
- Ground black pepper

How To

1. Peel the orange and cut each of them in 4:5 crosswise slices
2. Transfer to a shallow serving dish and sprinkle vinegar, oregano and olive oil
3. Toss well
4. Chill for 30 minutes
5. Arrange the sliced-up onion and black olives on top
6. Decorate well and sprinkle some chives on top with a grind of fresh pepper

7. Enjoy!

Nutrition Values (Per Serving)

- Calories: 120
- Fat: 6g
- Carbohydrates: 20g
- Protein: 2g

Avocado and Cilantro Medley

Serving: 6

Prep Time: 10 minutes

Cook Time: 0 minutes

SmartPoints: 2

Ingredients

- 2 avocados - peeled, pitted and diced
- 1 chopped up sweet onion
- 1 green bell pepper (chopped up)
- 1 large sized chopped up ripe tomato
- ¼ cup of chopped up fresh cilantro
- ½ of a juiced lime
- Salt as needed
- Pepper as needed

How To

1. Take a medium sized bowl and add onion, avocados, tomato, bell pepper, lime juice and cilantro
2. Give it a toss and season with salt and pepper
3. Serve chilled!

Nutrition Values (Per Serving)

- Calories: 126
- Fat: 10g
- Carbohydrates: 10g
- Protein: 2g

Chapter 9: Vegetarian/Vegan Recipes

Cha-Ching Tortilla Pizza

Serving: 4

Prep Time: 10 minutes

Cook Time: 35 minutes

SmartPoints: 2

Ingredients

- 4 sprays of cooking spray
- 2 medium peppers, deseeded and sliced
- 1 small red onion cut up into 12 wedges
- 2 medium courgette cup up into slices
- 12 cherry tomatoes halved
- 4 weight watchers white wrap
- 4 tablespoon of tomato puree
- ½ a teaspoon of dried oregano
- 8 pitted olives (soaked in brine)
- 4 ounce of low fat grated cheese
- 10 leaves of fresh basil
- 1 portion of rocket

How To

1. Preheat your oven to 392-degree Fahrenheit

2. Take a baking tray and mist with cooking spray
3. Add the veggies except tomatoes
4. Mist the veggies with cooking spray and roast for 15 minutes
5. Add tomatoes and cook for 5:10 minutes more
6. Arrange the wraps on baking sheet
7. Mix tomato pure and oregano and spread over wraps
8. Top the veggies and olives and scatter over the cheese
9. Bake for 7:9 minutes more until the cheese melts and the bases are crisp
10. Top with basil leaves and handful of rocket, enjoy!

Nutrition Values (Per Serving)

- Calories: 220
- Fat: 11g
- Carbohydrates: 22g
- Protein: 10g

Vegan Butter Balls

Serving: 4

Prep Time: 10 minutes

Cook Time: 0 minutes

SmartPoints: 3

Ingredients

- 12 pieces of diced and pitted dates
- 1/3 cup of unsweetened shredded coconut
- 2 and a ½ tablespoon of almond butter

How To

1. Take a bowl and add the dates, coconut and almond flour
2. Give it a nice mix
3. Use the mixture to form balls
4. Store the balls and chill them
5. Enjoy!

Nutrition Values (Per Serving)

- Calories: 62
- Fat: 3g
- Carbohydrates: 8g
- Protein: 1g

Respectable Avocado Spread

Serving: 4

Prep Time: 10 minutes

Cook Time: 0 minutes

SmartPoints: 2

Ingredients

- 1 halved and pitted avocado
- 2 tablespoons of chopped fresh parsley
- 1 and a ½ teaspoon of extra virgin olive oil
- ½ a lemon juice
- ½ a teaspoon of salt
- ½ a teaspoon of ground black pepper
- ½ a teaspoon of onion powder
- ½ a teaspoon of garlic powder

How To

1. Scoop out the avocado flesh into a bowl
2. Add lemon juice, parsley, olive oil, salt, onion powder, garlic and pepper
3. Mix well and mash the mixture using potato masher
4. Serve the avocado spread as you like
5. Enjoy!

Nutrition Values (Per Serving)

- Calories: 170
- Fat: 10g
- Carbohydrates: 16g
- Protein: 5g

Beet and Mushroom Avocado Salad

Serving: 4

Prep Time: 10 minutes

Cook Time: 20 minutes

SmartPoints: 2

Ingredients

- 4 medium sized Portobello mushroom caps
- ¼ cup of lemon juice
- 3 tablespoon of olive oil
- 1 small shallots finely chopped up
- 5 ounce of baby kale
- 8 ounces of precooked, chopped up beets
- 2 thinly sliced ripe avocados

How To

1. Take a large sized rimmed baking sheet and spray Portobello mushroom caps with cooking spray
2. Sprinkle ½ a teaspoon of salt
3. Add mushroom to baking sheet and bake for 20 minutes at 450-degree Fahrenheit
4. Take a bowl and whisk in lemon juice, olive oil, shallot, ¼ teaspoon of salt, ¼ teaspoon of pepper
5. Add half of the beets and baby kale and toss

6. Divide the mixture amongst serving plates and top with avocado, mushroom

7. Serve with dressing and enjoy!

Nutrition Values (Per Serving)

- Calories: 370
- Fat: 26g
- Carbohydrates: 32g
- Protein: 7g

Magnificent Bean Balls

Serving: 30

Prep Time: 10 minutes

Cook Time: 0 minutes

SmartPoints: 2

Ingredients

- ½ a cup of dates
- ½ a cup of dried berries and cherries
- ½ a cup of ground almonds
- 2 tablespoons of cocoa
- 3 and a ¾ cups of Black beans
- 1 small orange zest

As topping

- Cocoa
- Coconut
- Toasted Pistachios

How To

1. Take a food processor and add dates, ground almond, cocoa, cherries, black bean and orange zest
2. Process well until finely chopped up
3. Use your hand to make balls out of the mixture into balls
4. Garnish the balls with toasted cocoa, coconut and pistachios

5. Serve and enjoy!

Nutrition Values (Per Serving)

- Calories: 366
- Fat: 14g
- Carbohydrates: 96g
- Protein: 8g

Crispy Potatoes with Vegan Sauce

Serving: 4

Prep Time: 15 minutes

Cook Time: 30 minutes

SmartPoints: 1

Ingredients

- 2 pound of mixed and halved baby potatoes
- 3 tablespoon of canola oil
- 1 cup of raw unsalted cashews soaked overnight
- 3 tablespoon of lemon juice
- ½ a teaspoon of chili powder
- ½ a teaspoon of sweet paprika
- ½ a teaspoon of garlic powder
- 1 teaspoon of Coarse sea salt
- ¼ cup of nutritional yeast
- ½ of a jalapeno chili, chopped and seeded

How To

1. Preheat your oven to 450-degree Fahrenheit
2. Take a bowl and add ½ teaspoon of salt, ¼ teaspoon of pepper, oil and mix
3. Take a rimmed baking sheet and spread potatoes evenly
4. Roast for 30 minutes

5. Take a blender and add lemon juice, chili powder, paprika, cashews, cumin, garlic powder, yeast, jalapeno and sea salt
6. Add 1 cup of water
7. Mix well to puree
8. Transfer the mix to a 2-quart saucepan and simmer over low heat for 5 minutes
9. Transfer the sauce to a bowl and serve with roast potatoes

Nutrition Values (Per Serving)

- Calories: 380
- Fat: 18g
- Carbohydrates: 47g
- Protein: 10

Zucchini "Pizza" Fancy Boats

Serving: 4

Prep Time: 10 minutes

Cook Time: 25 minutes

SmartPoints: 3

Ingredients

- 4 pieces of medium zucchini
- ½ a cup of Whole30 compliant Marinara sauce/tomato sauce
- 1/4 sliced red onion
- ¼ cup of chopped kalamata olives
- ½ a cup of sliced cherry tomatoes
- 2 tablespoons of fresh basil

How To

1. Preheat your oven to 400-degree Fahrenheit
2. Cut up the Zucchini half-lengthwise and shape them in boats
3. Take a bowl and add tomato sauce
4. Spread 1 layer of the sauce on top of each boat and top with onion, tomato and olives
5. Bake for 20:25 minutes until the Zucchini are tender
6. Top with basil and serve!

Nutrition Values (Per Serving)

- Calories: 278
- Fat: 20g
- Carbohydrates: 10g
- Protein: 15g

Friendly Heirloom Carrots

Serving: 3-4

Prep Time: 10 minutes

Cook Time: 45 minutes

SmartPoints: 1

Ingredients

- 1 bunch of fine heirloom carrots
- 1 tablespoon of fresh thyme leaves
- ½ a tablespoon of coconut oil
- 1 tablespoon of date paste
- 1/8 cup of fresh squeeze orange juices
- 1/8 teaspoon of sea salt
- Salt as needed

How To

1. Preheat your oven to 350-degree Fahrenheit
2. Wash the carrots and discard the green pieces
3. Take a small sized bowl and add coconut oil, orange juice, salt and date paste
4. Pour the mixture over carrots and spread on a large sized baking sheet
5. Sprinkle thyme and roast for 45 minutes
6. Sprinkle salt on top and enjoy!

Nutrition Values (Per Serving)

- Calories: 70
- Fat: 3g
- Carbohydrates: 11g
- Protein: 1g

Chapter 10: Dessert Recipes

Fried Apple Slices

Serving: 4

Prep Time: 10 minutes

Cook Time: 10 minutes

SmartPoints: 1

Ingredients

- ½ a cup of coconut oil
- ¼ cup of date paste
- 2 tablespoon of ground cinnamon
- 4 pieces of Granny Smith Apples, peeled, sliced and cored

How To

1. *Take a large sized skillet and place it over medium heat*
2. *Add oil and allow the oil to heat up*
3. *Stir in cinnamon and date paste into the oil*
4. *Add cut up apples and cook for 5:8 minutes until crispy*
5. *Enjoy!*

Nutrition Values (Per Serving)

- Calories: 368
- Fat: 23g
- Carbohydrates: 44g
- Protein: 1g

Easy to Make Carrot Balls

Serving: 10

Prep Time: 10 minutes

Cook Time: 0 minutes

SmartPoints: 2

Ingredients

- 6 pieces of pitted Medrol dates
- 1 finely grated carrot
- ¼ cup of raw walnuts
- ¼ cup of unsweetened finely shredded coconut
- 1 teaspoon of nutmeg
- 1/8 teaspoon of sea salt

How To

1. Take a food processor and add dates, ¼ cup of grated carrots, salt coconut, nutmeg
2. Mix well and puree the mixture
3. Add the walnuts and remaining ¼ cup of carrots
4. Pulse the mixture until you have a clunky texture
5. Form balls using your hand and roll them up in coconut
6. Top with carrots and chill
7. Enjoy!

Nutrition Values (Per Serving)

- Calories: 326
- Fat: 16g
- Carbohydrates: 42g
- Protein: 3g

The Mean Green Smoothie

Serving: 1

Prep Time: 10 minutes

Cook Time: 0 minutes

SmartPoints: 1

Ingredients

- 1 cup of frozen mixed berries
- ½ a cup of baby spinach leaves
- 2 tablespoon of fresh orange juice
- 2 tablespoons of water
- 1 medium sized ripe banana sliced up

How To

1. Open up the lid of your food processor
2. Add all of the listed ingredients into the blender/food processor
3. Blend everything well until a smooth consistency comes
4. Serve chilled!

Nutrition Values (Per Serving)

- Calories: 29
- Fat: 4g
- Carbohydrates: 54g

- Protein: 18g

Very Zesty Lemon Cheesecake

Serving: 8

Prep Time: 20 minutes

Cook Time: 60 minutes

SmartPoints: 6

Ingredients

- 4 sprays of cooking spray
- 12 pieces of ginger and lemon cookies
- 1 ounce of low fat spread, melted
- 2 zests of lemon
- 4 tablespoons of juice
- 6-ounce low fat soft cheese
- 7 ounces of Quark
- 3 medium raw eggs whole
- 1 teaspoon of level vanilla extract
- 2 teaspoons of corn flour
- 1 and a 1/3 ounce of Agave nectar
- 5 fresh sprigs of mint
- 1 portion of raspberries
- 1 tub of medium Fat Free Natural Fromager Frais

How To

1. *Preheat your oven to 320-degree Fahrenheit*
2. *Take a 7-inch cake tin and grease with cooking spray*

3. Put cookies in a sealed plastic bag a crush using a rolling pin to fine crumbs

4. Transfer to a bowl with melted spread

5. Press into your greased cake tin and make the base

6. Chill until the remaining ingredients are prepared

7. Put lemon zest and juice, quark, soft cheese, Fromager Frais, vanilla, eggs, corn flour and agave to a large bowl

8. Whisk until smooth and pour the batter into cake tin, bake for 1 hour

9. Turn the oven off and open the door, leave for 15 minutes

10. Remove the cake and allow it to cool

11. Decorate with lemon slices, mint and raspberries

12. Enjoy!

Nutrition Values (Per Serving)

- Calories: 199
- Fat: 13g
- Carbohydrates: 18g
- Protein: 3g

Watermelon Sorbet

Serving: 4

Prep Time: 10 minutes

Chill Time: 20 hours

SmartPoints: 2

Ingredients

- 4 cups of seedless watermelon chunks
- ¼ cup of superfine sugar
- 2 tablespoon of lime juice

How To

1. Add the listed ingredients to a blender and puree them

2. Transfer to a freezer with tight-fitting lid and freeze covered until the mixture resembles set gelatin, it should take about 4:6 hours

3. Puree the watermelon mix in batches and return them to a container, freeze overnight

4. Allow the sorbet to stand for 5 minutes and serve!

Nutrition Values (Per Serving)

- Calories: 91
- Fat: 0g

- Carbohydrates: 25g
- Protein: 1g

Palatable Carrot Cake

Serving: 4

Prep Time: 10 minutes

Cook Time: 0 minutes

SmartPoints: 5

Ingredients

- ¾ cup of all-purpose flour
- ½ a cup of yellow cornmeal
- 1 and a ½ teaspoon of baking powder
- ½ a teaspoon of ground cinnamon
- ¼ teaspoon salt
- ½ a cup of thawed frozen apple juice concentrate
- ¼ cup of fat free milk
- 4 tablespoon of canola oil
- 1 large egg
- 2 tablespoons of brown sugar
- 1 cup of shredded carrots
- ½ a cup of raisin

For frosting

- ½ a cup of light cream cheese
- 1 tablespoon of honey

How To

1. Preheat your oven to 375-degree Fahrenheit
2. Spray a 9-inch Bundt pan with cooking spray
3. Take a bowl and whisk in flour, cornmeal, baking powder, salt and cinnamon
4. Use an electric mixer to beat apple juice concentrate, milk, oil, egg, brown sugar in a large bowl
5. Beat in carrots and raisins and reduce the mixer speed
6. Add flour mixture and keep beating until blended well
7. Scrape the mixture into your pan
8. Bake for 35:40 minutes and check using a tooth pick, it should come out clean
9. Combine cream cheese and honey in a food processor
10. Invert the cake onto a plate and use a narrow spatula to spread the frosting over the cake
11. Enjoy!

Nutrition Values (Per Serving)

- Calories: 155
- Fat: 1g
- Carbohydrates: 15
- Protein: 3g

The Weight Watchers Brown Betty

Serving: 4

Prep Time: 10 minutes

Cook Time: 45 minutes

SmartPoints: 3

Ingredients

- 4 slices of low calorie whole wheat bread, torn into pieces
- 2 tablespoons of light brown sugar
- 1 teaspoon of ground cinnamon
- 4 golden apples, peeled, cored and sliced
- 2 teaspoons of butter, cut up into pieces
- 1/3 cup of water

How To

1. Preheat your oven to 375-degree Fahrenheit
2. Take the shallow casserole dish and grease with cooking spray
3. Put toast in food processor or blender and pulse until coarse crumb forms
4. Transfer to a small bowl
5. Add brown sugar and cinnamon and toss well
6. Spread half of the apples in prepped casserole
7. Sprinkle evenly with half of crumb mixture

8. Spread the rest of the apples on top and cover with remaining crumb mixture

9. Dot evenly butter and drizzle water over

10. Bake for 45 minutes and enjoy!

Nutrition Values (Per Serving)

- Calories: 177
- Fat: 3g
- Carbohydrates: 40g
- Protein: 3g

Amazing Baked Apples

Serving: 1

Prep Time: 5 minutes

Cook Time: 20 minutes

SmartPoints: 0

Ingredients

- 1 piece of Fuji apple
- Raisins as needed
- Cinnamon as needed

How To

1. *Preheat your oven to 347-degree Fahrenheit*
2. *Core the apples*
3. *Stuff them with cinnamon and raisins*
4. *Transfer to the oven and bake for 20 minutes*
5. *Serve and enjoy!*

Nutrition Values (Per Serving)

- Calories: 95
- Fat: 0.27g
- Carbohydrates: 42g
- Protein: 0.43g

Rice Pudding and Golden Raisins

Serving: 4

Prep Time: 10 minutes

Cook Time: 25 minutes

SmartPoints: 8

Ingredients

- 2 cups of fat free milk
- ¼ cup of sugar
- 2 tablespoons of water
- 1 and a 1/3 cup of Arborio rice
- 2 large eggs
- ¼ cup of golden raisins
- 1 teaspoon of vanilla extract
- Pinch of cinnamon
- 4 teaspoons of butter

How To

1. Add 1 cup of milk, sugar, water in a small saucepan
2. Bring to mix to a boil
3. Stir in rice and lower down the heat to low, simmer for 30 minutes making sure to keep stirring it from time to time
4. Preheat your oven to 325-degree Fahrenheit

5. Spray 1 and a ½ quart baking dish with nonstick cooking spray

6. Add 1 cup of milk, eggs, vanilla, raisins and cinnamon to a medium bowl

7. Stir in rice

8. Pour the mix into baking dish and dot with butter

9. Bake for 25 minutes

10. Enjoy!

Nutrition Values (Per Serving)

- Calories: 238
- Fat: 2g
- Carbohydrates: 43g
- Protein: 7g

Conclusion

I can't express how honored I am to think that you found my book interesting and informative enough to read it all through to the end.

I thank you again for purchasing this book and I hope that you had as much fun reading it as I had writing it.

I bid you farewell and encourage you to move forward with your amazing weight watchers journey!

Appendix

list of the most common ingredients and their SP (Old Program)

Below is a list of the most common ingredients alongside their associated Smart Point for your convenience.

Food with 0 SP

- Coffee
- Banana
- Apple
- Strawberries
- Chicken Breast
- Salad
- Blueberries
- Grapes
- Tomatoes
- Watermelon
- Egg White
- Lettuce
- Deli Sliced Turkey Breast
- Baby Carrots
- Orange
- Cucumber

- Broccoli
- Water
- Green Beans
- Pineapple
- Corn on The Cob (medium)
- Cherries
- Cantaloupe
- Spinach
- Fresh Fruit
- Raspberries
- Shrimp
- Asparagus
- Celery
- Cherry Tomatoes
- Carrots
- Yogurt
- Peach
- Sweet Red Potatoes
- Pear
- Salsa
- Tuna
- Diet Coke
- Mushrooms
- Onions
- Black Beans
- Blackberries
- Zucchini
- Grape Tomatoes
- Mixed Berries

- Grapefruit
- Nectarine
- Mango
- Mustard

Food with 1 SP

- Sugar
- Almond Milk
- Egg
- Guacamole
- Half and Half
- Salad Dressing

Food with 2 SP

- Cream
- Avocado
- 1 Slice Of Bread
- Scrambled Egg with milk/ butter
- Luncheon Meat, deli sliced or ham (2 ounce)
- 2 t tablespoon of Hummus

Food with 3 SP

- Milk Skimmed
- 1 tablespoon of Mayonnaise
- Chocolate Chip Cookies
- Sweet potatoes ½ a cup
- 3 ounce of boneless Pork Chop
- 1 ounce of flour Tortilla
- Italian Salad Dressing 2 tablespoon

- 3 slices of cooked Turkey Bacon
- 1 cup of Cottage Cheese
- Ounce of crumbled Feta

Food with 4 SP

- Olive Oil
- American Cheese 1 slice
- Low Fat Milk 1%, 1 Cup
- Cheddar Cheese 1 ounce
- Red Wine 5 ounce
- ¼ cup of Almond
- 5 ounce of White Wine
- Tortilla Chips 1 ounce
- Shredded Cheddar Cheese
- 1 tablespoon of honey
- 102 ounce of English Muffin
- Mashed Potatoes

Food with 5 SP

- Butter
- 3 Slices of Cooked Bacon
- Reduced Fat Milk 1 Cup
- Cooked Oatmeal 1 cup
- Plain Baked Potato, 6 ounce
- Regular Beer, 12 ounce
- 1 cup of cooked regular/ whole wheat pasta
- Hamburger Bun
- Ranch Salad Dressing
- Any type of Bagel (2 ounce)

- 1 cup of Spaghetti

Food With 6+ SP

- White Rice (6)
- Brown Rice (6)
- Peanut Butter 2 tablespoon (6)
- 1 Whole Cup Of Milk (7)
- 20 ounce of French Fries (13)
- 1 cup of cooked Quinoa (6)

Ingredients and Food Groups That are Zeroed Out in the new Freestyle Plan.

- Peas such as chick peas, sugar snap peas, black eyed etc.
- Beans such as black beans, kidney beans, pinto beans, fat free refried beans, soy beans, sprouts etc.
- Lentils
- Corn such as baby corn, sweet corn, corn on the cob
- Skinless Chicken Breast
- Skinless Turkey Breast
- Tofu
- Egg and Egg Whites
- Fish and Shellfish
- Yogurt
- Lean Ground Beef
- Non Fat and Plain Greek Yogurt
- All Fruits
- All Vegetables

To give you a more detailed look at the list, the following now hold a 0 SmartPoint value.

- Yogurt
- Plain Yogurt
- Greek Yogurt
- Watermelon
- Watercress
- Water Chestnuts
- Stir Fried Vegetables
- Mixed Vegetables
- Sticks of Vegetables
- Turnips
- Turkey Breast
- Turkey Breast Tenderloin
- Ground Turkey Breast
- Tomato
- Tomato Sauce
- Tofu
- Taro
- Tangerine
- Tangelo
- Star fruit
- Winter and Summer Squash
- Spinach
- Shellfish
- Shallots
- Scallions
- Sauerkraut
- Chicken aSatay
- Sashimi
- Salsa

- Salad
- Lentils
- Lime
- Lettuce
- Litchi
- Mangoes
- Mung Dal
- Mushroom Caps
- Nectarine
- Okra
- Onions
- Orange
- Parsley
- Pea Shoot
- Peaches
- Pear
- Pepper
- Pickles
- Pineapple
- Plums
- Pomegranate Seeds
- Pomelo
- Pumpkin
- Pumpkin Puree
- Radish
- Salad Mixed Greens
- Salad Three Bean
- Lemon Zest
- Leek
- Kiwifruit
- Jicama
- Jerk Chicken Breast

- Jackfruit
- Heart of Palm
- Guava
- Mixed Baby Greens
- Ginger Root
- Grape Fruit
- Fruit Cup
- Fruit Cocktail
- Fish Fillet
- Fruit
- Fish
- Figs
- Fennel
- Escarole
- Endive
- Egg Whites
- Eggs
- Apples
- Arrowroot
- Applesauce
- Artichoke
- Artichoke Hearts
- Bamboo Shoots
- Banana
- Beans
- Beets
- Blueberries
- Blackberries
- Broccoli
- Brussels
- Cabbage
- Carrots

- Cauliflower
- Cherries
- Chicken Breast
- Clementine
- Cucumber
- Dragon Fruit
- Egg Substitute
- Dates

And a few more.

Made in the USA
Lexington, KY
04 May 2018